# CONTENTS

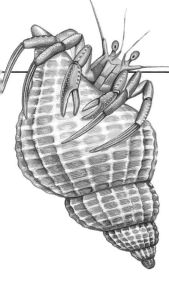

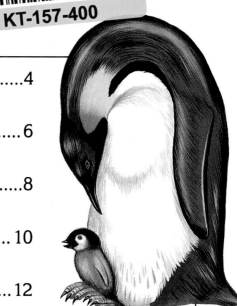

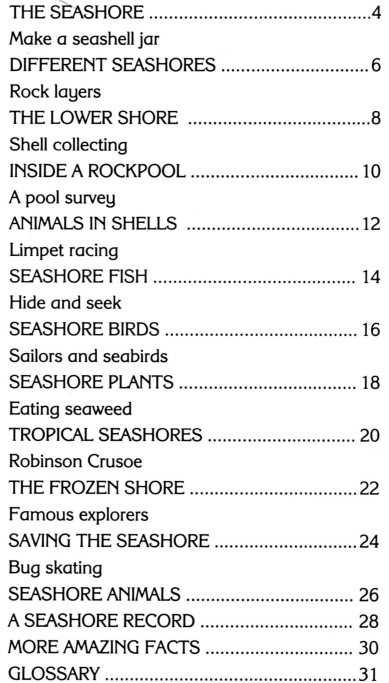

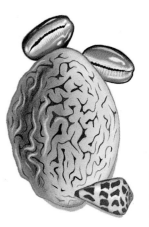

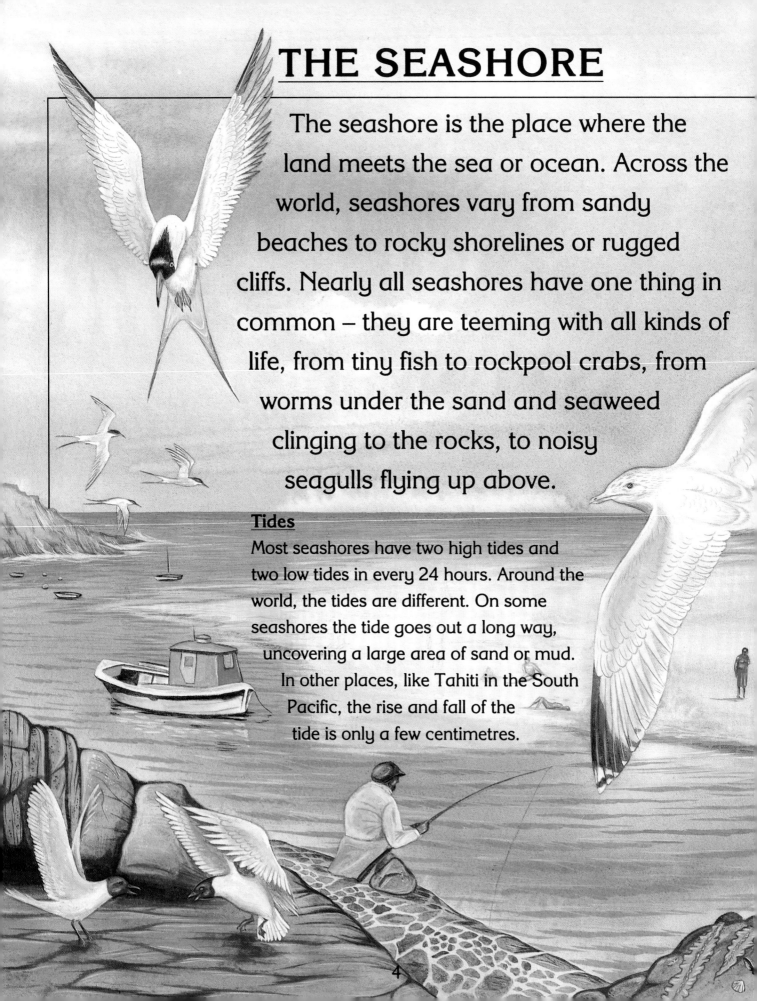

# THE SEASHORE

The seashore is the place where the land meets the sea or ocean. Across the world, seashores vary from sandy beaches to rocky shorelines or rugged cliffs. Nearly all seashores have one thing in common – they are teeming with all kinds of life, from tiny fish to rockpool crabs, from worms under the sand and seaweed clinging to the rocks, to noisy seagulls flying up above.

## Tides

Most seashores have two high tides and two low tides in every 24 hours. Around the world, the tides are different. On some seashores the tide goes out a long way, uncovering a large area of sand or mud. In other places, like Tahiti in the South Pacific, the rise and fall of the tide is only a few centimetres.

# FASCINATING FACTS ABOUT

# THE SEASHORE

## JANE WALKER

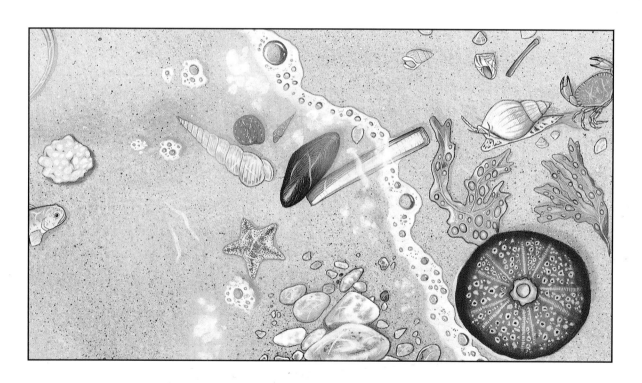

**Franklin Watts**

London • Sydney

# INTRODUCTION

Seashores around the world are home to a huge number of plants and animals. Some bury themselves under the wet sand, while others live on the rocky clifftops, or hide in deep rockpools left behind when the tide goes out. In this book we look at some of this wildlife, and see how it lives and feeds along the seashore. You can have fun with a number of **Practical Projects**, learn how to write your own **Seashore Diary** and discover a lot of **Amazing Facts** about the seashore.

© Aladdin Books Ltd 1993
New edition published in 2003

Designed and produced by
Aladdin Books Ltd
28 Percy Street
London W1T 2BZ

First published in
Great Britain in 1993 by
Franklin Watts
96 Leonard Street
London EC2A 4XD

Design:      David West
             Children's Book
             Design
Designer:    Flick Killerby
Editor:      Richard Green
Illustrators: Justine Peek
             David Marshall
Cartoons:    Tony Kenyon
Consultant:  Joyce Pope

ISBN 0 7496 5123 7

Printed in UAE

A CIP catalogue record
for this book is available
from the British Library

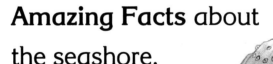

The world's highest SEA CLIFFS in Hawaii
have a drop of over 1,000 metres
to the sea.

## Make a seashell jar

Collect as many different shells as you can find.
Cover the outside of a glass jar with plaster of
Paris. Make sure you do this on some newspaper
as it can be quite messy. Gently press the shells
into the mixture and leave it to set hard. Later,
you can varnish the outside of the jar. You can
also try covering a plant pot or a small box in
the same way.

The SEASHORE is an enjoyable place to visit.
Surfers ride the waves, fishermen dig for worms
in the sand and children paddle in the sea, or
look for rockpool creatures with nets and buckets.

# DIFFERENT SEASHORES

Some seashores are covered with fine powdery sand, or the sand may be rough and grainy. Other shores have rocks and pebbles, or tiny round stones called shingle. These different seashores have all been formed by the sea. The sea is so strong that it wears away rocks and cliffs, and is constantly changing the shape of the shore.

### Sand dunes
As the wind blows from the sea across the beach, it pushes the sand into piles called sand dunes. Sand dunes are sometimes so big that they can cover the tops of churches or even whole villages.

*Waves can wear away so much rock that they eventually cut one section away from the cliffs to form a SEA STACK.*

## From rock to sand

As waves crash down on the seashore, small pieces of rocks and pebbles are tossed around and thrown back onto the shore. Over time, the rocks and pebbles become smaller and smoother. Eventually, they are worn away so much that they turn into fine grains of sand. The sea finally leaves, or deposits, the sand along the shore to form a beach.

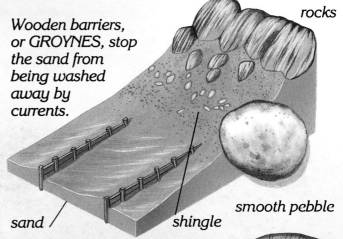

*Wooden barriers, or GROYNES, stop the sand from being washed away by currents.*

rocks

sand / shingle

smooth pebble

## Rock layers

Over millions of years, many dead animals and plants have settled down in layers on the seabed. As more and more layers piled up, they squeezed down on the trapped remains of plants and animals, turning them into rock. These remains are called fossils. Some seashore fossils show creatures that lived over 200 million years ago. Fossils are often found in a rock called limestone.

# THE LOWER SHORE

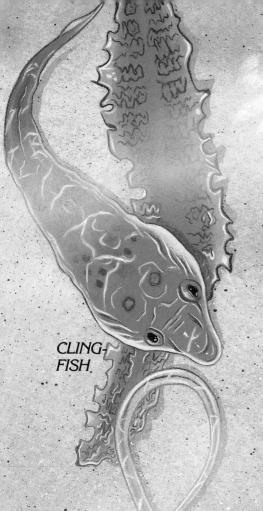

CLING-
FISH

WHELK
EGG
CASE

PIPEFISH

SAND
GOBY

When the tide goes out and uncovers the lower shore, you can find lots of different creatures both on the sand and below the surface. Small fish, like gobies and pipefish, swim in sandy pools. Crabs scuttle across the surface looking for food, or bury themselves in the cool, wet sand. The common whelk, or buckie, lays its yellow eggs in muddy sand or gravel along the lower shore.

### Beneath the surface

Many creatures live below the seashore's surface. Worm-like shapes, called casts, lie on the wet sand. They are made by lugworms which live in burrows underneath. A razorshell uses its foot to dig down in the sand, and can disappear from view in a few seconds. The sand goby lives in sandy pools, and uses its fins to bury itself in the sand.

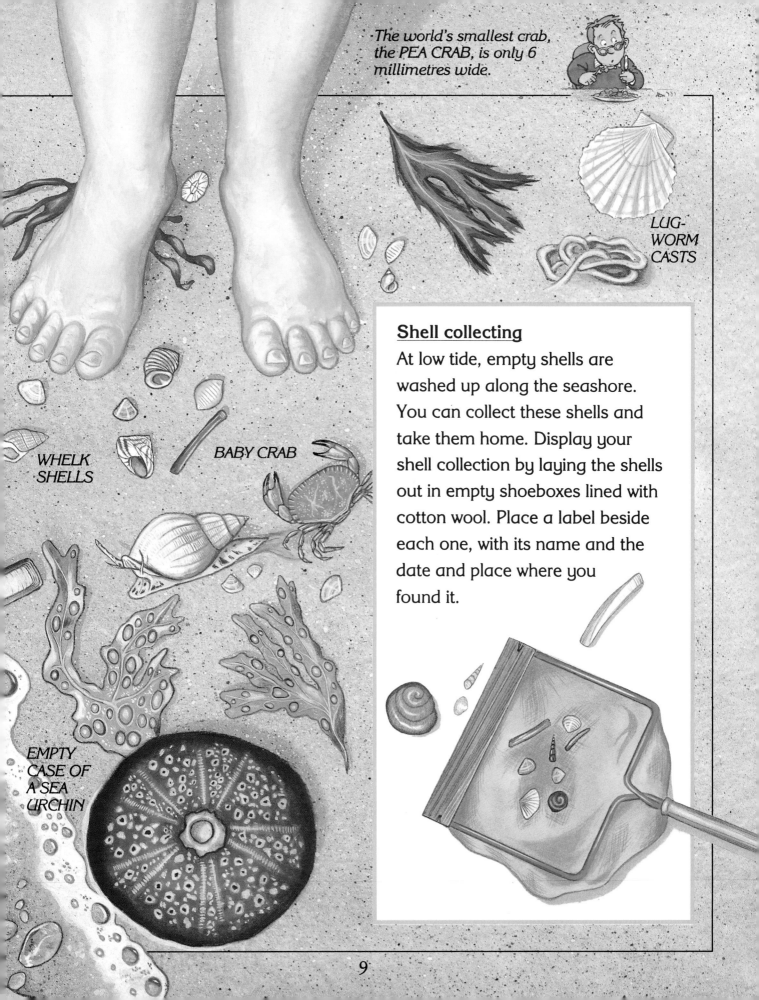

*The world's smallest crab, the PEA CRAB, is only 6 millimetres wide.*

LUG-WORM CASTS

## Shell collecting

At low tide, empty shells are washed up along the seashore. You can collect these shells and take them home. Display your shell collection by laying the shells out in empty shoeboxes lined with cotton wool. Place a label beside each one, with its name and the date and place where you found it.

WHELK SHELLS

BABY CRAB

EMPTY CASE OF A SEA URCHIN

Along a rocky seashore there are dozens of rockpools filled with seawater at low tide. Rockpools are interesting places to explore. Limpets and winkles feed on tiny pieces of seaweed, and in turn provide food for flesh-eating animals such as starfish and whelks. Small fish and crabs hunt shrimps and other tiny creatures hiding among the seaweed.

### Rockpool hunters

In deeper pools, hunting fish like sea scorpions and weever fish lie in wait for any small fish that swims past. Dog whelks crawl over the rocks in search of a meal of barnacles or mussels. Sea anemones wait patiently to trap shrimps and small fish in their tentacles.

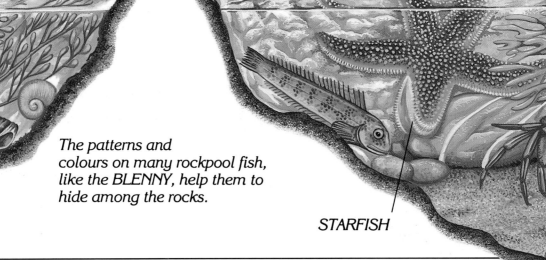

LIMPET

*The patterns and colours on many rockpool fish, like the BLENNY, help them to hide among the rocks.*

STARFISH

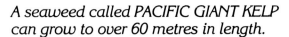

## A pool survey

Next time you visit the seashore, try making a survey of the life inside a rockpool. Sketch the outline of a rockpool and look closely at each part (and under the seaweed) to find out which creatures and plants live in it. Add these to your rockpool sketch.

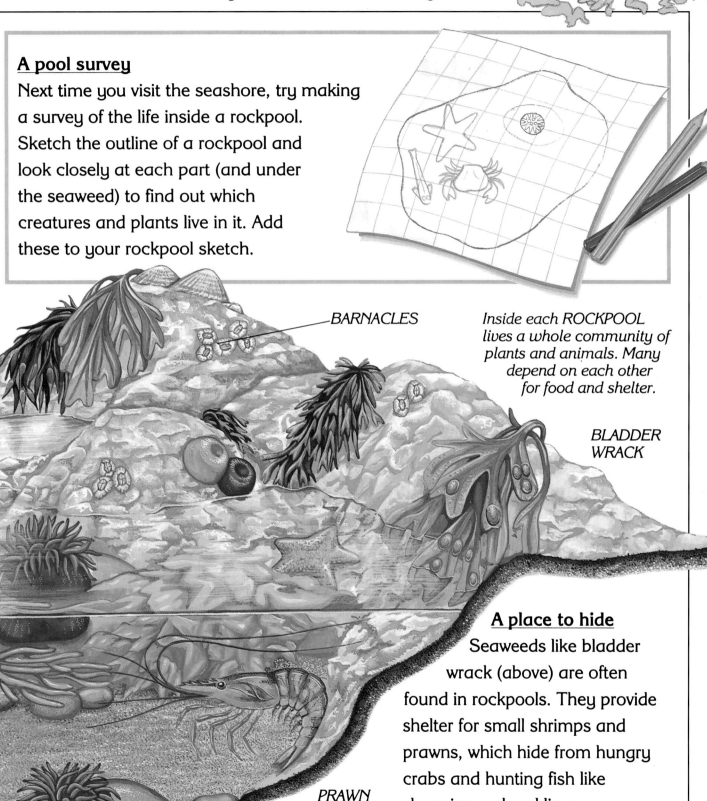

BARNACLES

*Inside each ROCKPOOL
lives a whole community of
plants and animals. Many
depend on each other
for food and shelter.*

BLADDER
WRACK

PRAWN

SEA ANEMONE

## A place to hide

Seaweeds like bladder wrack (above) are often found in rockpools. They provide shelter for small shrimps and prawns, which hide from hungry crabs and hunting fish like shannies and rocklings.

# ANIMALS IN SHELLS

Many of the creatures living on the seashore have a hard shell to protect their soft bodies from the waves, and from being dried out by the Sun and wind. Animals like crabs, lobsters and prawns have a hard outer shell and several pairs of legs with joints. Most crabs and lobsters have five pairs of legs – four pairs for moving and a fifth pair called pincers. Crabs use their pincers to defend themselves and to tear off pieces of food.

### Snails of the seashore

Many seashore creatures, such as whelks, periwinkles and topshells (above), are related to land snails. They have a coiled shell which surrounds the soft body of the animal inside. These sea snails move by sliding along on a single foot of muscle.

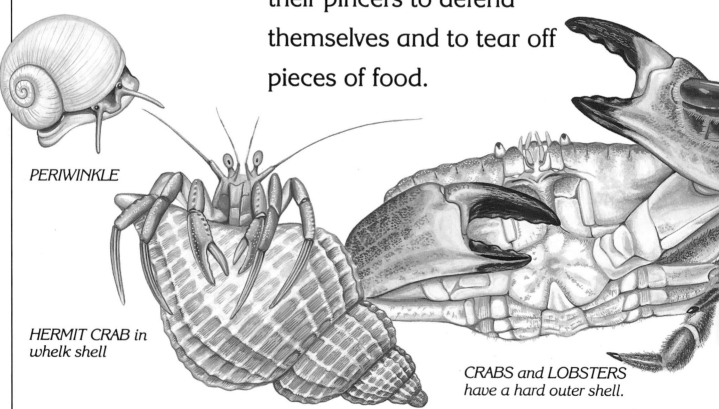

*PERIWINKLE*

*HERMIT CRAB in whelk shell*

*CRABS and LOBSTERS have a hard outer shell.*

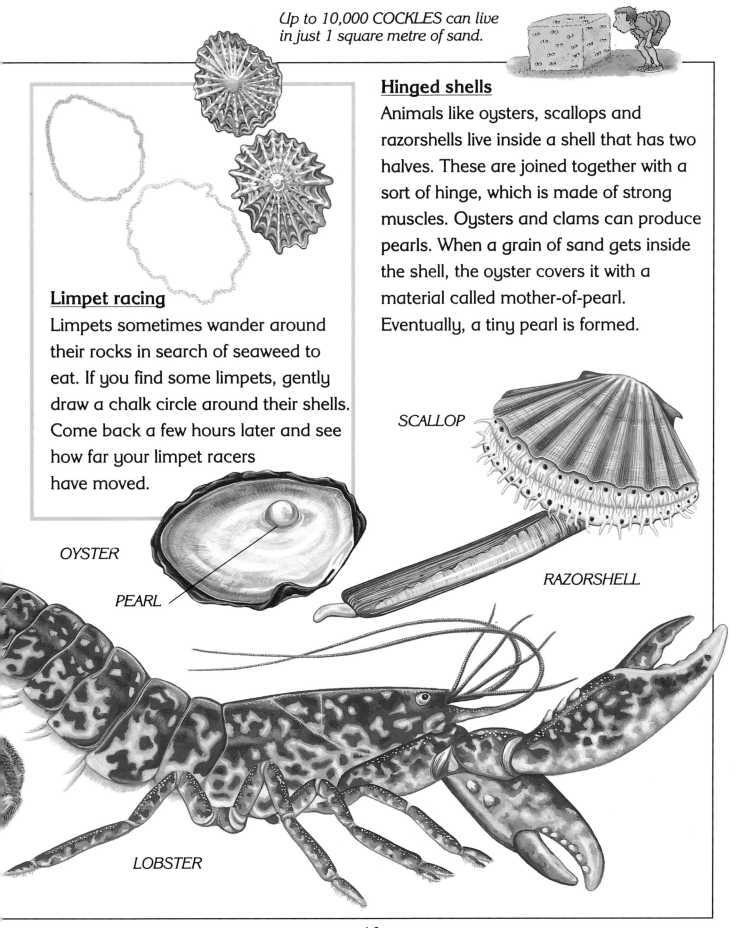

## Hinged shells

Animals like oysters, scallops and razorshells live inside a shell that has two halves. These are joined together with a sort of hinge, which is made of strong muscles. Oysters and clams can produce pearls. When a grain of sand gets inside the shell, the oyster covers it with a material called mother-of-pearl. Eventually, a tiny pearl is formed.

## Limpet racing

Limpets sometimes wander around their rocks in search of seaweed to eat. If you find some limpets, gently draw a chalk circle around their shells. Come back a few hours later and see how far your limpet racers have moved.

OYSTER

PEARL

SCALLOP

RAZORSHELL

LOBSTER

13

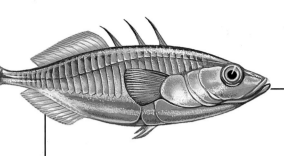

# SEASHORE FISH

Seashore fish live in the rockpools and shallow puddles left behind when the tide goes out. Waves can wash these fish onto the rocks or sand. The clingfish and lumpsucker fish have special disc-shaped suckers to help them cling to the rocks. Another danger facing these fish are hunters looking for food. Scavenging gulls and eels are always ready to gobble up any small seashore fish.

### Food for fish

Small fish, such as sticklebacks (above), shannies and rocklings, feed on prawns and shrimps. They hunt in rockpools and shallow water and at low tide.

*EEL hide under stones and seaweeds in shallow pools on rocky seashores.*

### Hide and seek

You can make a game of hide and seek with cardboard fish on a coloured background. Cut out some fish shapes and paint a different background on four large squares of stiff paper or card. Now paint your fish to match the backgrounds. Lay the fish on their surroundings and see if your friends can find them. The person who finds

### Flatfish

Larger fish, such as wrasse, tub gurnard and sea-bass, usually live in deeper water out to sea, but sometimes visit the shallow waters along the seashore when the tide comes in. Fish like dabs, plaice and flounders have thin, flat bodies and are known as flatfish. The colourings on the skin of many flatfish match the sandy surroundings of the seabed. This helps the fish to hide from their enemies, but it also makes them difficult to be noticed on the seashore.

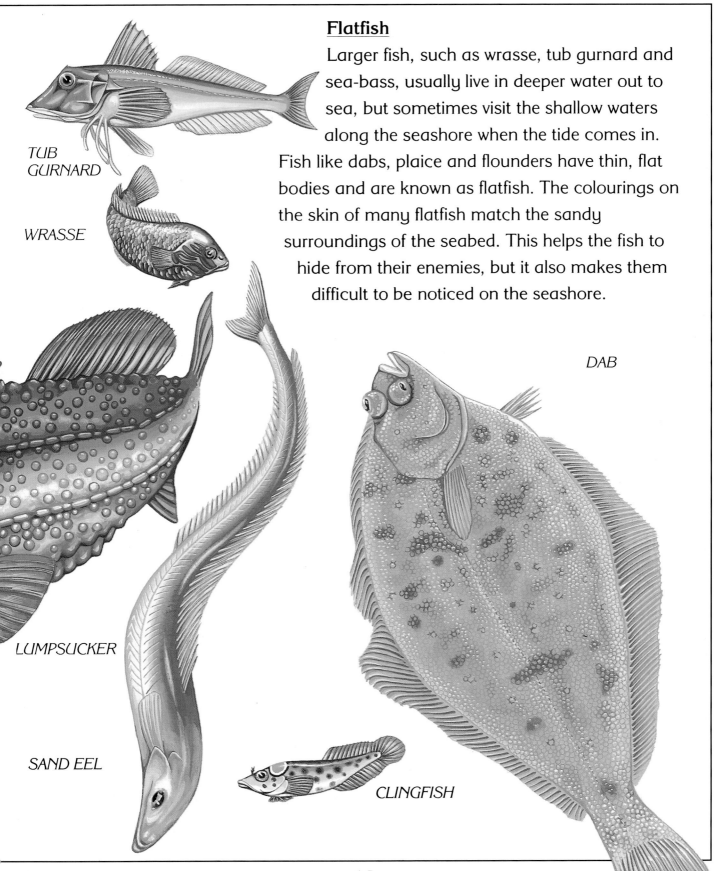

TUB GURNARD

WRASSE

LUMPSUCKER

SAND EEL

CLINGFISH

DAB

# SEASHORE BIRDS

On the steep, rocky cliffs along many seashores, thousands of seabirds live together in family groups called colonies. Razorbills and kittiwakes lay their eggs on the bare ledges. A guillemot egg is pear-shaped to stop it from rolling off the rocky ledge. Puffins dig burrows for their eggs and chicks in the soft soil on top of cliffs.

ARCTIC TERN

### Migrating seabirds

In one year the Arctic tern can fly over 25,000 kilometres from its northern summer home to its Antarctic winter home, and back again.

PUFFIN

RAZORBILL AND EGG

### Birds on the beach

Not all seabirds lay their eggs on rocky cliffs. The little, or least, tern lays its eggs on quiet beaches or sand dunes. The eggs and newly hatched chicks are speckled and sandy-coloured to match their surroundings.

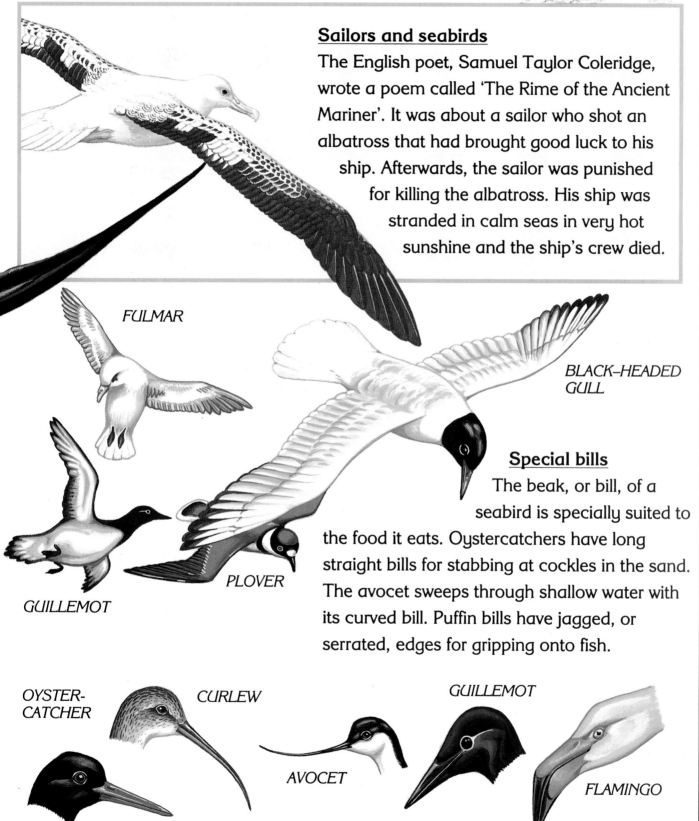

## Sailors and seabirds

The English poet, Samuel Taylor Coleridge, wrote a poem called 'The Rime of the Ancient Mariner'. It was about a sailor who shot an albatross that had brought good luck to his ship. Afterwards, the sailor was punished for killing the albatross. His ship was stranded in calm seas in very hot sunshine and the ship's crew died.

*FULMAR*

*BLACK–HEADED GULL*

## Special bills

The beak, or bill, of a seabird is specially suited to the food it eats. Oystercatchers have long straight bills for stabbing at cockles in the sand. The avocet sweeps through shallow water with its curved bill. Puffin bills have jagged, or serrated, edges for gripping onto fish.

*GUILLEMOT*

*PLOVER*

*OYSTER-CATCHER*

*CURLEW*

*GUILLEMOT*

*AVOCET*

*FLAMINGO*

# SEASHORE PLANTS

Seashore plants have to survive harsh conditions such as strong winds, salty spray and soft sand. Plants like the sea holly have waxy leaves to stop them from drying out. Up on the clifftop, the sea pink (or thrift) and sea campion are small and bushy with deep roots to avoid being blown away by the wind.

## Seashore stripes

Sometimes coloured stripes of seaweed lie along the shore. These are made by the three groups of seaweed – green, red and brown.

## Seaweeds

Seaweeds are found on seashores throughout the world. They do not need roots like land plants because they get food straight from the water. Seaweeds have a special part called a holdfast to grip onto rocks. The leaves, or fronds, of some seaweeds like bladder wrack (see page 11) have sacs of gas to help the plants stay upright in the water.

*SEA LETTUCE*

*PLOCAMIUM*

## In the dunes

Many dune plants, like marram grass and sand sedge, have long, creeping roots to anchor them into the sand. The roots can also find water deep down below the dry surface. Colourful plants, like sea bindweed, grow along the ground and help protect the dunes by preventing sand from being blown away by the wind.

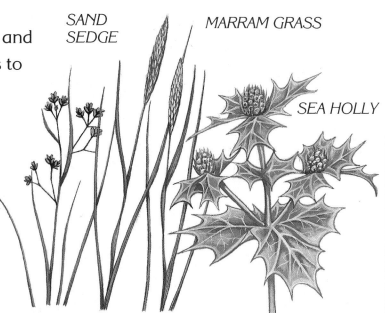

SAND SEDGE

MARRAM GRASS

SEA HOLLY

CARRAGHEEN

OARWEED

## Eating seaweed

Seaweeds are filled with vitamins and a mineral called iodine. They are a common food in countries like China and Japan. Seaweed can be eaten raw in salad or cooked as a vegetable. Seaweed soup is popular in Japan. In Wales, a red seaweed is used to make a special kind of dish called laver bread.

# TROPICAL SEASHORES

The tropical seashore, with its warm seas and hot sunshine, is sometimes lined with rows of coconut trees bent into strange shapes by strong winds. Pieces of coral and the shells of cowries and spotted topshells are washed up on the fine, white sand. On other shores, fiddler crabs and odd fish called mudskippers search for food and shade in the cool, wet mud of the mangrove swamps.

*BRAIN CORAL*

## Corals

Coral is found in warm, shallow water in tropical seas. It is made by the skeletons of millions of tiny animals called polyps. When these creatures die, their remains build up to form a coral reef. Coral reefs provide homes to thousands of fish, starfish and sea anemones.

## Robinson Crusoe

Daniel Defoe wrote a book about a sailor who was shipwrecked on a desert island. The sailor's name was Robinson Crusoe. He lived alone on the island for over 20 years. One day, Robinson Crusoe finds the footprints of another person on the beach. When he meets the other man he calls him Friday. About three years later, Robinson Crusoe and Friday are rescued by a passing ship.

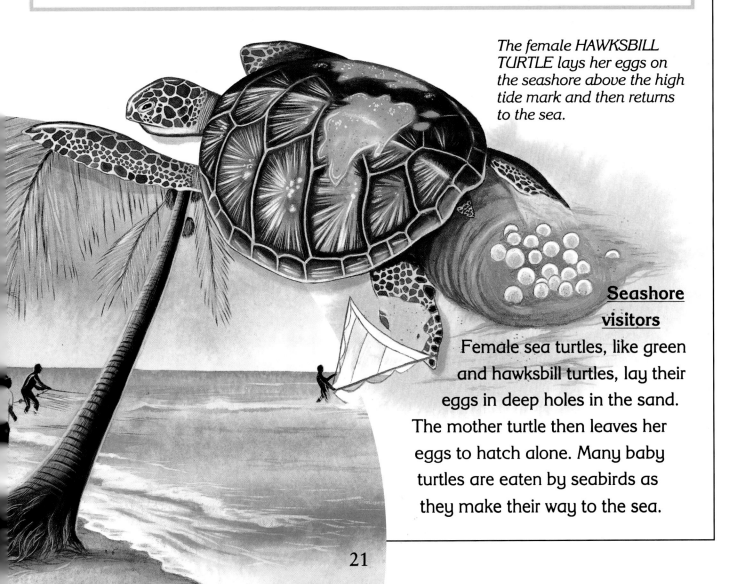

*The female HAWKSBILL TURTLE lays her eggs on the seashore above the high tide mark and then returns to the sea.*

### Seashore visitors

Female sea turtles, like green and hawksbill turtles, lay their eggs in deep holes in the sand. The mother turtle then leaves her eggs to hatch alone. Many baby turtles are eaten by seabirds as they make their way to the sea.

# THE FROZEN SHORE

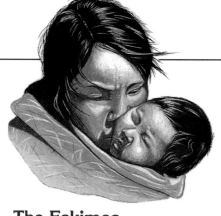

In the far north of the world, around the North Pole, stretch the bare shores of the Arctic Ocean. This seashore stays frozen for about 8 months each year. At the opposite end of the world lies the vast icy continent of Antarctica, covered by a huge sheet of ice and surrounded by sea on all sides.

### The Eskimos

The people who live in the lands around the Arctic Ocean are called Eskimos. In the past, they lived in igloo homes made from blocks of ice. Today, Eskimos live in modern houses in towns and small settlements.

*Male EMPEROR PENGUIN and chick*

### The Antarctic

The weather in the Antarctic is so cold that animals like elephant seals (below) and penguins have a thick layer of fat, called blubber, to help them stay warm. Penguins can't fly, and look clumsy on the ice, but in the sea they swim very gracefully and at great speed. Emperor penguins are the largest kind of penguin. After the females lay their eggs, the males stand in a huddle, keeping the eggs warm on their feet for more than 2 months.

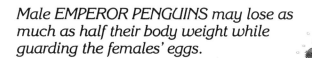

*Male EMPEROR PENGUINS may lose as much as half their body weight while guarding the females' eggs.*

### The Arctic

Polar bears spend much of their time hunting seals at the edge of the ice. They creep up on the seals as they bask in the sunshine or catch them as they come up to breathe at a hole in the ice. During the summer months, millions of seabirds such as terns, skuas and gulls, fly to the Arctic seashore to build their nests and raise their young.

*ARCTIC SKUA*

*The WALRUS has long tusks that it uses for defence and to drag itself along the ice. Its thick layer of blubber helps to keep it warm.*

*POLAR BEARS*

### Famous explorers

The polar lands were some of the last places in the world to be reached by human beings. Captain James Cook may have seen Antarctica as long ago as 1774. In 1911, the Norwegian explorer, Roald Amundsen, was the first person to reach the South Pole. He arrived just ahead of a group of British explorers, led by Captain Robert F. Scott.

# SAVING THE SEASHORE

The seashore is constantly under attack – from people and from the sea itself, as waves gradually wear away rocks and cliffs. Yet one of the greatest threats to the seashore comes from pollution. Chemicals, sewage, oil and rubbish are dumped into the sea. Eventually, this rubbish is washed onto the seashore, where it damages or kills many seashore plants and animals.

## Rubbish

Empty plastic bottles, old rusty tins, rubber tyres and broken glass are some of the rubbish you can easily find on most seashores. We must keep the seashore clean by picking up litter and not dropping any ourselves.

## Oily beaches

In 1989, the oil tanker Exxon Valdez ran aground in Alaska, USA, spilling 50 million litres of oil. Millions of fish and over 300,000 seabirds died. Oil slicks poison fish, and smother seabirds, seals and turtles. Rescue workers (shown left) help save seabirds when their feathers become clogged with oil.

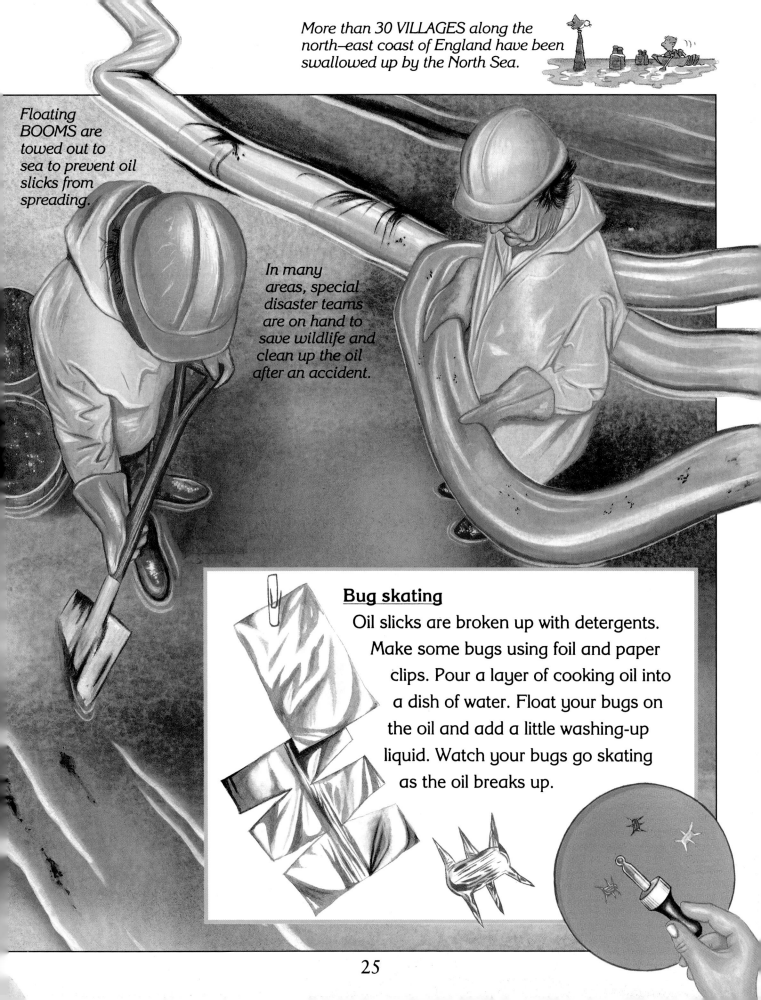

More than 30 VILLAGES along the
north–east coast of England have been
swallowed up by the North Sea.

Floating
BOOMS are
towed out to
sea to prevent oil
slicks from
spreading.

In many
areas, special
disaster teams
are on hand to
save wildlife and
clean up the oil
after an accident.

### Bug skating

Oil slicks are broken up with detergents.
Make some bugs using foil and paper
clips. Pour a layer of cooking oil into
a dish of water. Float your bugs on
the oil and add a little washing-up
liquid. Watch your bugs go skating
as the oil breaks up.

# SEASHORE ANIMALS

Do you know which seashore creatures are related to each other? Scientists have separated seashore animals into different groups. The animals in one group are usually similar to each other. Crabs and lobsters belong to one group, while starfish and sea urchins belong to another group. But sometimes animals in the same group look quite different from each other. Can you believe that a mussel and an octopus are part of the same group?

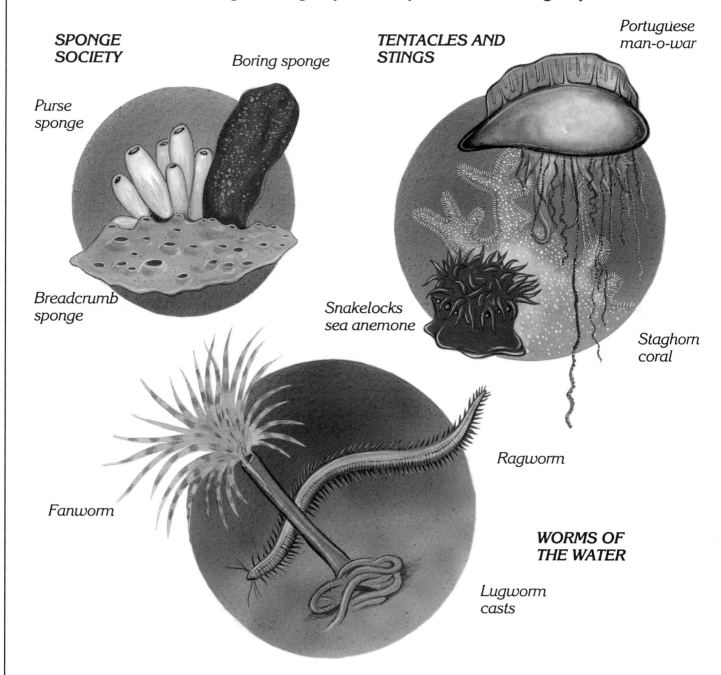

**SPONGE SOCIETY**

Boring sponge

Purse sponge

Breadcrumb sponge

**TENTACLES AND STINGS**

Portuguese man-o-war

Snakelocks sea anemone

Staghorn coral

Fanworm

Ragworm

**WORMS OF THE WATER**

Lugworm casts

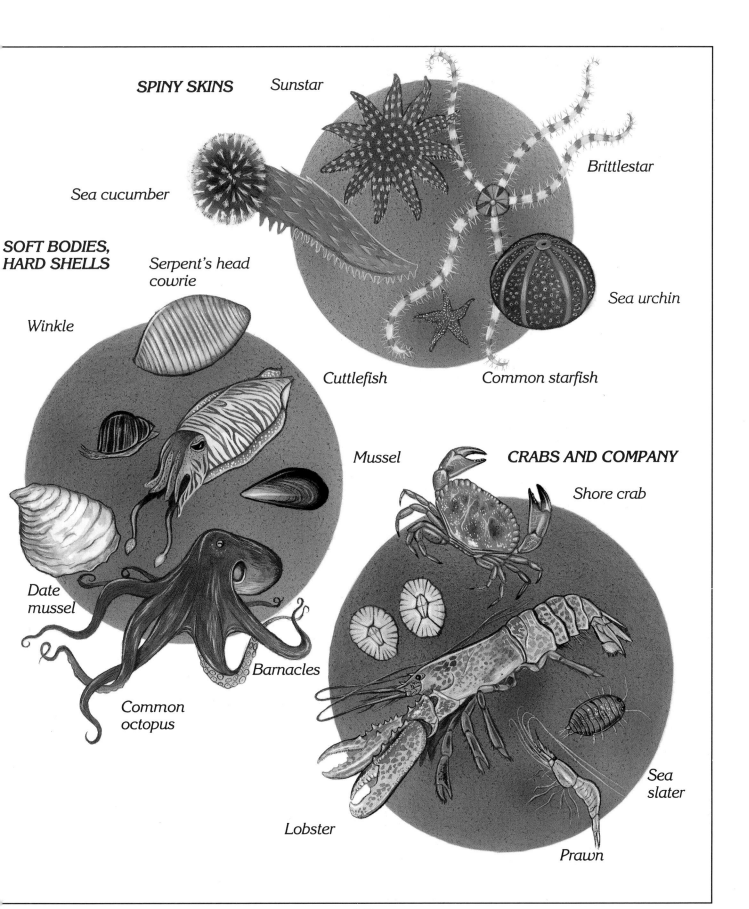

**SPINY SKINS**

Sunstar

Sea cucumber

Brittlestar

Sea urchin

Cuttlefish

Common starfish

**SOFT BODIES, HARD SHELLS**

Serpent's head cowrie

Winkle

Mussel

**CRABS AND COMPANY**

Shore crab

Date mussel

Barnacles

Common octopus

Lobster

Sea slater

Prawn

# A SEASHORE RECORD

You can keep a record of the many different kinds of animals and plants along the seashore by creating your own seashore diary. Using a simple exercise book, you can draw pictures of the creatures and plants that you find. Don't forget to colour or paint them later.

Remember to write down in which part of the seashore you found your creatures, as well as their names (if you know them). You can look up some of the names in a reference book later, or ask an adult to help you.

## Shells
Try to find out which animals lived in the empty shells you collect on the seashore. Does the shell have a hinge, or is it coiled like a snail shell?

## Safety at the seashore
The seashore is a beautiful and interesting place, but it can also be dangerous. Be careful of tides and strong waves – always tell an adult when you go near the water. Wear shoes to protect your feet from sharp rocks and rubbish, and take care not to get sunburnt – it can spoil a fun day at the seaside.

LOWER SHORE

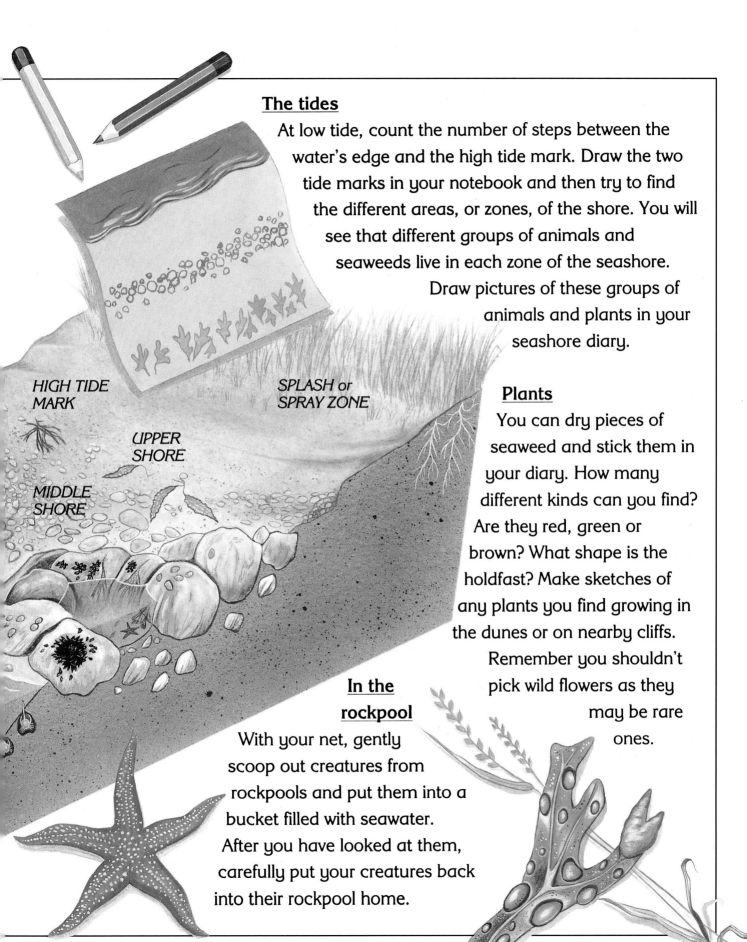

### The tides

At low tide, count the number of steps between the water's edge and the high tide mark. Draw the two tide marks in your notebook and then try to find the different areas, or zones, of the shore. You will see that different groups of animals and seaweeds live in each zone of the seashore. Draw pictures of these groups of animals and plants in your seashore diary.

*HIGH TIDE MARK*

*SPLASH or SPRAY ZONE*

*UPPER SHORE*

*MIDDLE SHORE*

### Plants

You can dry pieces of seaweed and stick them in your diary. How many different kinds can you find? Are they red, green or brown? What shape is the holdfast? Make sketches of any plants you find growing in the dunes or on nearby cliffs. Remember you shouldn't pick wild flowers as they may be rare ones.

### In the rockpool

With your net, gently scoop out creatures from rockpools and put them into a bucket filled with seawater. After you have looked at them, carefully put your creatures back into their rockpool home.

# MORE AMAZING FACTS

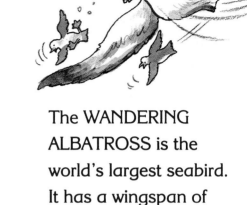

The BEADLET ANEMONE has a circle of 24 tiny blue spots, like beads, around the bottom of its tentacles.

The WANDERING ALBATROSS is the world's largest seabird. It has a wingspan of nearly 4 metres.

DOG WHELKS change colour according to the colour of the food they eat.

The EDIBLE CRAB is also known as the PIE–CRUST CRAB because its shell looks like the pastry from the top of a pie.

HERMIT CRABS do not have their own hard shell to protect their soft bodies so they live in the empty shells of other seashore creatures.

SEA LEMONS lay a long string of eggs that may contain as many as half a million eggs.

# GLOSSARY

**BILL** The beak of a bird.

**COLONY** A large group of birds living together, often on rocky cliffs.

**CURRENT** When an area of sea moves in a particular direction, caused by the shape of the shore and the wind.

**DUNES** Sand blown into piles by the wind.

**FOSSIL** The remains of a once-living plant or animal preserved in rock.

**FRONDS** The leaves of a seaweed.

**GROYNES** Wooden barriers on sandy beaches to prevent sand from being washed away by the current.

**HIGH TIDE MARK** The highest place that the sea reaches when the tide comes in.

**MIGRATION** Regular movements of animals such as birds and fish from one place to another.

**OIL SLICK** A large pool of oil which floats on the surface of the sea.

**SCAVENGER** An animal that clears up the remains of another animal's meal.

**SEA STACK** A section of rock which has been separated from the cliffs by the sea and waves.

**SHELL** The hard outer covering of sea creatures such as crabs, prawns and whelks, which protects their soft bodies.

**SHINGLE** Small, smooth pieces of gravel or pebbles, usually found on the upper part of the seashore.

**TENTACLE** A soft, finger-like strand near the the mouth of an animal like a sea anemone, or octopus. Tentacles are used to catch food.

**TIDE** The regular rise and fall of the sea, which floods and then uncovers the seashore normally twice every day.

**WINGSPAN** The distance from one tip of a bird's wing to the tip of the other.

**ZONES** Different areas on the seashore created by the rise and fall of the tide. Different animals live in different zones.

# INDEX